A SUMMARY OF MARK LEIBOVICH'S

SUMMARY, REVIEW & ANALYSIS

THIS TOWN

TWO PARTIES AND A FUNERAL

MARK LEIBOVICH

Note to Readers: We encourage you to first order a copy of Mark Leibovich's full book, *This Town: Two Parties and a Funeral?Plus, Plenty of Valet Parking!- inAmerica's Gilded Capital* before you read this unofficial Book Summary & Review. Most readers use this guide by first reading a chapter from the full copy, and then reading the corresponding section from this Book Summary & Review. Others prefer to read the entire book from cover-to-cover, and then review using this review and analysis.

Other Amazon Kindle Ebooks from *Save Time Summaries:*

Summary of *The Unwinding: An Inner History of the New America -- George Packer -- Summary & Analysis*

Summary of *Team of Rivals: The Political Genius of Abraham Lincoln by Doris Kearns Goodwin -- Chapter-by-Chapter Guide & Analysis*

Summary of *The Hit by David Baldacci -- Summary & Study Guide (Will Robie)*

Summary of *Unbroken -- A World War II Story of Survival, Resilience, and Redemption by Laura Hillenbrand*

Summary of Mark Owen's *No Easy Day: The Firsthand Account of the Mission That Killed Osama Bin Laden*

Summary of Stephen Covey's *The 7 Habits of Highly Effective People*

Save Time Summaries
Las Vegas, NV 89128
savetimesummaries@gmail.com

TABLE OF CONTENTS

OVERVIEW 1

ABOUT THE AUTHOR OF *THIS TOWN* 5

PROLOGUE 6

CHAPTER ONE: HEAVEN'S GREEN ROOM 8

CHAPTER TWO: SUCK-UP CITY 11

CHAPTER THREE: THREE SENATORS FOR
OUR TIMES 14

CHAPTER FOUR: THE ENTOURAGE 17

CHAPTER FIVE: EMBEDDING 20

CHAPTER SIX: "THANK YOU FOR YOUR
SERVICE" 23

CHAPTER SEVEN: THE ROACH MOTEL OF
POWER 27

CHAPTER EIGHT: HOW IT WORKS 30

CHAPTER NINE: PERFORMING ARTS 33

CHAPTER TEN: ANARCHY IN THE QUIET
CAR 36

CHAPTER ELEVEN: THE PRESIDENTIAL
CAMPAIGN: THIS MOVIE AGAIN 38

CHAPTER TWELVE: THE PRESIDENTIAL
CAMPAIGN: SADDENED, TROUBLED 41

CHAPTER THIRTEEN: THE PRESIDENTIAL CAMPAIGN: BELLY FLOPS, BOURBON CHOCOLATE TRUFFLES, AND WONDERFUL RUINS 44

CHAPTER FOURTEEN: THE LAST PARTY 47

EPILOGUE...49

PUTTING IT TOGETHER 52

OVERVIEW

Washington, D.C. has been described as a poli-media-corporate pigpen, where just about everyone is, has been, or will be at the trough. It is hard to tell when sentiments, emotions, and feelings are genuine. It appears that, by and large, even those expressions of sincere love and affection are really a product of self-interest and of the need to maintain appearances.

A clear-eyed, cynical, gossipy portrayal of the DC elite – journalistic, political, and business – Mark Leibovich's *This Town* is also in places hilarious. The biographical sketches of the good and the great are usually done with a cool evenhandedness, describing their shortcomings and qualities. Their interactions are equally well rendered as they battle in their quests to be at the top of the pecking order. Neither the current nor the "former" (a reference to past office holders now making zillions as lobbyists) are spared from Leibovich's humorous analysis.

57th Presidential Inauguration, 21 January 2013. Photo Courtesy of CC

The Washington story is punctuated by two kinds of events: funerals and parties. The funerals of the members of The Club (those who belong and "matter") provide special occasions for other members of The Club to gather. Parties also, of course, bring members together and seem to occur with stunning frequency in DC. This phenomenon neatly encapsulates the seeming paradoxes and contradictions of "This Town"—although polar opposites, funerals and parties serve the same purpose of lubricating the interactions of DC movers and shakers, past, present, and future.

The book captures the zeitgeist of present-day DC, a place where ideals and high-minded public service is corrupted by the lure of money. Some of the culture's fiercest critics arrive in town and are coopted by a system that systematically sucks up to them, heaping them with adulation and holding out a future of wealth as lobbyists if they play by the rules.

As it happens, the perfect example is the Obama phenomenon. Full of hope and high ideals, the Obama administration was filled with acerbic critics of the capital's culture and modus operandi before coming to Washington. The book shows how this same administration is forced to make a series of compromises in order to survive in this political climate, fighting an uphill battle to implement its stated ideals of the campaign. Many of the administration's main operatives and leading lights are likewise seduced by huge compensations paid out by the very same corporations that they formerly criticized as having caused major damage, such as BP or Goldman Sachs.

Personality-driven yet ultimately insightful and utterly engaging, *This Town* delivers a stunning critique – rarely delivered from a self-professed Club member such as Leibovich – of the incestuous relationships that serve only to enrich and entrench DC's

3

power-brokers at the expense of any
meaningful reform.

About The Author of *This Town*

"Mark Leibovich is an American journalist and author. He is the chief national correspondent for The New York Times Magazine, based in Washington, D.C. He is known for his profiles on political and media figures." (Wikipedia.com)

PROLOGUE

Summary

The funeral service for acclaimed DC journalist Tim Russert is used to introduce the reader to the capital's elites and their ways of life. Because Russert was one of the most prestigious and influential journalists in Washington, the funeral is attended by the capital's most important politicians and lobbyists, as well as by fellow journalists. It's a rare chance to network, but this can't be done overtly or with too much zeal on account of the occasion.

The author admits to being part of that circle of power and influence that is DC's elite. He also claims to be very comfortable with his life in DC, and to perhaps have a less-than-objective perspective because of it.

It is June 2008, and the funeral is attended not only by top government officials about to end their terms of office, but also by top advisors to the about-to-be anointed Democratic candidate for the presidency, Barack Obama. As such, Robert Gibbs and David Axelrod hold some of the most sought-after hands to be shaken.

6

In a place where pecking order is everything, Tim Russert was at the very top. He possessed the attributes necessary to become part of what is variously called "The Club," "Permanent Washington," "The Beltway Establishment," "The Gang of 600," and, of course, "This Town." People did not mess with Tim. He was personable and charming in a non-elitist sort of way, and he had gravitas.

Nor is it wise for Club members to mess with Bill and Hillary Clinton, both of whom are in attendance of course. A cable news reporter's recent derogatory comment about Chelsea Clinton leads to his suspension from the network. He has hardly been heard from since.

KEY TAKE-AWAYS

• Who is up and who is down is everything in a place where power and influence are the coin of the realm.

• In spite of outward appearances of partisanship, "The Town" is a self-serving tightly knit community.

Chapter One: HEAVEN'S GREEN ROOM

Summary

A living legend, Tim Russert died at the prime of his influence of a coronary thrombosis while working at his NBC studio. He managed to hide his incredible ambition beneath a veneer of everyman modesty, apparently a quality that incredibly ambitious Washington types must possess.

Appearances on his TV show, *Meet the Press*, were proof of having made it. In a town where exposure and prestige are everything, Russert held the key to belonging to "The Club," and, as such, was lionized and sought after as few other individuals were—"adored-in that unmistakable vintage of Washington 'adored' that incorporated fear and need and sucking up," as Leibovich puts it.

As a result, the procession at his funeral includes most of the great and the good, including presidential candidates Obama and John McCain, who are seated together for the occasion. Just about everybody bestows a variety of extraordinary accolades upon Russert. Nevertheless, none of it is really about him (according to the author, Russert would have known this better than anyone), but rather it is about those left behind and their quest to get ahead.

Tim Russert's son, Luke Russert, gives an excellent eulogy. We are also introduced to a series of Washington characters. There is Terry McAuliffe, the former Democratic National Committee chairman known as "The Macker" (but more importantly, the professional friend of former President Bill Clinton). Dubbed the best fundraiser in the universe by Al Gore, he once went so far as to leave his wife and his newborn child in the car (right after having picked them up from the hospital) in order to attend a fundraising event for the Democratic Party.

Rainbow at Tim Russert's funeral.

To add the cherry to the cake, a couple of spectacular rainbows make their appearance just as the procession of notables climbs atop the Kennedy center for a cocktail party, prompting Luke Russert to exclaim, "Is anyone still an atheist now?"

KEY TAKE-AWAY

• In Washington, even funerals and wakes (especially those of the most distinguished dead) are occasions to schmooze and network while keeping up appearances of grieving.

Chapter Two: SUCK-UP CITY

Summary

We meet Andrea Mitchell, a high-ranking member of "The Club." She is one of the premier members of the media, a TV anchorwoman who is held up as an example of integrity and competence. Additionally, she is also married to former Federal Reserve Chairman Alan Greenspan. But wait a minute, the Greenspan brand has been tarnished as of late. It is late 2008-early 2009, and the economy is in a free fall with many blaming Greenspan's Ayn-Randish libertarian free-market policies. Mitchell, much to her chagrin, is told by editors not to comment on the causes of the financial meltdown on account of conflict of interest. At the same time, she is given the freedom to discuss only the political implications of the crisis.

Meanwhile, DC is being rocked by the Obama phenomenon. Washington is accustomed to presidential candidates claiming in their campaigns to be outsiders who are coming to clean up the rotten capital—only to be coopted by the capital once elected. Could this time be different? The Obama people

11

seem particularly earnest in their genuine contempt for Washington's seamier side and culture of self-perpetuation, self-enrichment, celebrity madness, and sycophancy. But in spite of Obama and his crowd's contempt for Washington's ways, the media is in a frenzy of adulation over him that has not been seen since JFK. The Obama brand, in the words of a media pundit, is the best brand in the world.

Another character we are introduced to is Robert Barnett. The consummate insider, Barnett is so extraordinarily skillful and trusted that he manages to represent both sides of the same negotiation. Top media people hire him to negotiate their compensations; at the same time he represents the organizations that will hire those people. He is the go-to agent in negotiating amounts to be paid for the most sought-after political autobiographies, such as those of both Bill and Hillary Clinton.

Another archetypal character is Tamara Haddad. She is not a journalist, businessperson, philanthropist, producer, or party host, but she manages to do a little bit of each of those things. As Leibovich describes it, Haddad is a "full-service gatherer of friends of different persuasions unified by the fact that they in some way 'matter'." She is so good at this that she manages to get *Newsweek* a prized interview with Obama and his wife while traveling in Air Force One—with her on board, of course.

KEY TAKE-AWAYS

• DC is a cynical, hard-edged town where sentimentalism is a pose, where nostalgia has no place unless it is for public consumption, and where only the present matters.

• People skills and a great personality are at a premium in a place like DC.

Chapter Three: THREE SENATORS FOR OUR TIMES

Summary

Harry Reid, the Senate majority leader, is in some ways atypical of the elite in Washington. He neither looks nor acts the part. As the author eloquently describes it, Reid is "endowed with all the magnetism of a dried snail." But what he lacks in charisma is more than made up for by toughness and an extraordinary capacity to empathize and commiserate with fellow senators.

In one sense, he fits well into the Washington narrative; he had a hard-as-nails upbringing in the town of Searchlight, Nevada (population 539). His coal mining father committed suicide and Reid had to buy his mother false teeth. In his early youth, he became an amateur boxer and often ended up in street fights. Now he is in charge of a super majority in the Senate and is the point man for the Obama administration's ambitious legislative agenda.

Ideologically, Republican Senator Tom Coburn is at the opposite extreme to Reid.

He is an inspirational figure to the Tea Party movement, having championed many of their anti-spending positions long before they ever existed. He is one of the few authentic true abhorrers of Washington, of its corruption, and of its entrenched and self-perpetuating elites. To Coburn, Big Government is detestable, and market-friendly policies are the only policies worth espousing. Whether or not those views please anyone around him is of no consequence to him.

Even though Trent Lott is also a Republican, he is a very different type of Republican from Coburn. Lott may espouse many of the same ideological positions, but he is very much part of the entrenched elite in Washington. Years earlier, Coburn could not believe his ears when then-Senate majority leader Lott shot down Coburn's ideas, saying that they would have to wait until after the elections. For Coburn, putting elections before principle is sacrilege. After leaving the Senate, Lott became one of the premier lobbyists in town—in Washington parlance, a "former." As such, he is very much appreciated by the likes of Reid, who misses Lott's brand of pragmatic deal making in the Senate. One can surmise, however, that Coburn doesn't share Reid's sentiments.

KEY TAKE-AWAYS

- Washington is a curious mixture of extraordinary hypocrisy and cynicism coupled with, at times, genuine feelings among its members.

- Truman's dictum, "if you want a friend in Washington, get a dog," appears to be mostly, but not completely, true.

- Power is just as addictive as (if not more so than) drugs or gambling; often the effort to maintain power at any price leads to dysfunction.

Chapter Four: THE ENTOURAGE

Summary

Washington these days is in many ways run by people with no constitutional authority, but instead by lobbyists making oodles of money (even though the term "lobbyist" has become discredited) and high-powered journalists of the new media who want to not only influence, but also drive, events.

In addition, a new sort of celebrity has been born: the political advisor or consigliere. All of a sudden, the goings-on of Washington's denizens have become saleable news nationwide, no matter how trivial, tawdry, or superficial.

It was not always this way, of course. If embryonic versions of all of these phenomena were perhaps rearing their heads in the last century, it has only been in the last twenty to thirty years that they have evolved to become the present phenomena they are now.

Lobbyists, PR firms, and campaign firms used to resemble mom-and-pop outfits. With the advent of big money (particularly from corporations and Wall Street), lobbying, PR firms, and campaign firms have become full-blown industries that have made their leading practitioners fabulously wealthy.

Washington has become a topic a national entertainment topic resulting from the mixture of high-level sex scandals, the creation of political celebrities, and the new revolutionary media technologies. In this brave new world, journalists have become celebrities in their own right, even as they cover the comings and goings of This Town's political celebrities. The epitome of this brave new world is Politico's Mike Allen, publisher of the very latest news of all kinds—part of the secret being that you want to keep your name in print.

Political advisors have become Celebrity Operators, none more celebrated than James Carville and Mary Matalin. Despite being fierce partisan rivals, these two ended up marrying each other, underlining the suspicion that, beneath all the partisan conflict, the elites ultimately share an enduring interest in the status quo wherein they are top dogs.

KEY TAKE-AWAY

• Washington has been transmogrified from a sleepy town where the nation's business was transacted, into a celebrity-generating, entertainment-creating, media–absorbing, and money-distributing dynamo.

Chapter Five: EMBEDDING

Summary

This chapter describes the new type of journalism that exists in DC, with Mike Allen being its chief creator and purveyor. An obsessively private man, Allen's calling nonetheless dictates that he must constantly be in public (whether at meetings, news conferences, parties, get-togethers, and whatever other kind of important event conceivable). Whether he sleeps at all is a subject of speculation.

What he does with Playbook (the email publication that, at last count, has 100,000 subscribers and is read daily by the vast majority of Club members) is collate and distill the top stories from among the countless that are out there. In this sense, he follows what has already been sighted and, at the same time, gives leads for others to follow and report on. Moreover, speculation or gossip that frequently has no, or next to no, basis is given flight by its mere mention, and one suspects that it is mentioned because it has titillation value. For example, the prospect of Obama dumping Vice President Joe Biden in favor of

Hillary Clinton in 2012 was reported in Playbook, despite having been denied by a close Clinton aide before the speculation ever ran.

Allen is exceptionally considerate and thoughtful of others. He is also, according to those who know him best, genuine in his demonstrations of affection and thoughtfulness toward others. His outlook and perception of that which he covers (i.e., This Town) consist of respect and admiration for those in power; his motivation is to be present and to report on history being made. Criticized for "snowflake journalism" because of the evanescent nature of his reporting, many of the stories he reports on are what drives or feeds the DC scene. The combination of his manic personality—manic in terms of his capacity for work—and the new information technology embodied in the Internet has given rise to this prospective successor to Tim Russert. Allen is quickly becoming the king of the journalism hill in DC.

KEY TAKE-AWAYS

- It takes a special kind of talent, drive and vision to create a new standard of media coverage.

- The new instant-media coverage of DC is another example of IT playing a part in the transformation of a profession.

Chapter Six: "THANK YOU FOR YOUR SERVICE"

Summary

This chapter discusses Michael Hastings' *Rolling Stone* story about General Stanley McChrystal and his staff making various criticisms and dismissive comments in regards to some of the highest officials in government, including Biden. However, it was not the substance of the comments or whether they were accurate that was important. What mattered was that McChrystal and his people had been clumsy, imprudent, and naïve enough to have had their comments recorded by Hastings. The general had to resign.

A bitter controversy arose as to whether Hastings had been unethical in his dealings with the general and his staff. He was attacked as someone who had used his charm to ingratiate himself with McChrystal and his advisors, only to later publish their unguarded comments they had assumed to be in confidence. Those who scoffed at the criticism said that it's not a journalist's fault if those interviewed are so remarkably naïve as to be honest with a journalist and think themselves immune to exposure.

Regardless, where Hastings crossed a red line in regards to his standing in The Club was when he said explicitly that he had taken advantage of the general and his staff by gaining their confidence enough that they would make those comments in front of him. For most DC journalists today, it seems that playing by The Club's unspoken rules often takes precedence over investigative journalism and uncovering a genuine news story that serves to enlighten the public.

One of the biggest events in Washington's social calendar is the White House Correspondents' Association dinner. Initiated in 1920, it hasn't been missed by any president since 1924. A number of parties and gatherings have grown up alongside it, giving it the moniker "nerd prom." Beginning in the 1980s, and over time, the dinner and accompanying events started attracting Hollywood players and stars (as well as Wall Street bigwigs) in a smorgasbord of partying, eating, and drinking—"a multiday symbol of the city's self-intoxication."

President Obama cracks jokes at the White House
Correspondents Dinner

A number of anecdotes from Washington
insiders flow from these gatherings. One of
the most enlightening in this chapter is one
that involves McAuliffe, fundraiser
extraordinaire and close friend to President
Clinton. He wants to be ambassador to the
UK, but is afraid that the Senate might
object. He calls his Republican buddy
Mississippi Governor Haley Barbour, who
duly talks to then-Senate majority leader
Trent Lott. When asked about this, Barbour
assumes a faint air of being offended, as if
McAuliffe's association with Clinton may
possibly be an obstacle to a fine and
competent appointment. In reality, Lott told
Barbour to "tell that son of a bitch I'll walk
him to the airplane"—that way, Lott would
be rid of the best Democratic political
fundraiser ahead of the 2000 elections.

KEY TAKE-AWAYS

• Journalists and idealists in general are coopted and corrupted by DC, its glitter and glamour, its money, its freebies, and its parties.

• There is an unseemly juxtaposition between opulent DC celebrations and the economic bad times and disasters in the rest of the country.

• Cynicism and hypocrisy are rampant; money is the biggest motivator.

Chapter Seven: THE ROACH MOTEL OF POWER

Summary

Chris Dodd is the son of a senator and was a five-time senator and three-time congressman himself. He exemplifies perfectly how a card-carrying member of The Club can be at the same time the most unpopular incumbent. Realizing his reelection numbers were not good, he announced he would quit and start a line of work that would give back. He had once vowed to never become a lobbyist.

So what happened? He became a big-time lobbyist immediately after retiring.

Time after time, it's the same story. After decrying the hypocrisy, the bitter criticism, the corrupt influence on law makers, and how he or she is so tired of it, Congressperson X Senator Y becomes precisely one of those corrupting influencers. Idealists become "institutionalized" into the Washington culture.

Cashing in on former public service is, moreover, a thoroughly bipartisan affair. To top it all off, these former public servants will join outfits that push interests that are diametrically opposed to those causes they formerly championed as public servants. One of the most egregious examples is former Democratic Representative Dick Gephardt, House majority leader and two-time presidential candidate. A leading champion of organized labor, he became one of the prime lobbyists for huge corporations (among them Goldman Sachs, Boeing, Visa, and Spirit Aerosystems) whereby he was paid to advise on an antiunion campaign.

Needless to say, big-time lobbyists make big-time money, often in the eight-figure range. Although they are expensive, their services are very cost-effective for corporations that can benefit to the tune of tens of millions of dollars as a result of even the slightest of tweaks in a bill. As former Republican lobbyist and convicted felon Jack Abramoff put it, the moment he would subtly imply to an elected official that a lobbying job would be on offer after they leave office, "we own them."

KEY TAKE-AWAYS

• Money trumps principles almost every time.

• The hypocrisy of former elected officials who denounce special interest influence and then are later hired as lobbyists, under that or any other title, has no limits.

Chapter Eight: HOW IT WORKS

Summary

Leibovich was tasked with writing a story about Representative Darrell Issa. In the process he ran into Issa's press secretary, Kurt Bardella, a much more interesting character. Bardella was so interesting that Leibovich proposed to Bardella that he would write a book about Washington insiders featuring Bardella.

Bardella was a Korean orphan adopted by an American family, hence his name. He had a difficult upbringing because his adoptive parents divorced and his adoptive mother remarried.

Bardella is an unusual Washingtonian, not only because of his Asian origin, but especially because he does not hide his outsized ambition. He didn't attend college; instead, he worked for local politicians in California until he hooked up with a Republican who had made it into Congress. From there, he got himself hired by Issa, who became a sort of surrogate father to him, a situation that is not in the slightest bit unusual in DC.

A very effective press secretary, Bardella knew how to use the new media outlets such as Politico and Playbook to the fullest in order to advance his boss's career. Although Bardella has been characterized as brilliant, hard charging, and a workaholic, he has also been called immature and insecure. As he became ever more sought after as the press secretary of the head of a powerful Congressional committee, Bardella's immaturity became apparent through imprudent and arrogant comments that he made to a journalist that were subsequently used by Issa's critics against him. The result was that he almost got fired. Almost.

But Bardella had also offered Leibovich that he would share the daily email correspondence he had with members of the press so as to further the plan of a book that sought to portray the inner workings of Washington's political life and starred Bardella as a featured participant. Once it became known that emails were being shared without the knowledge of those who had sent them, Bardella landed in hot water again. Moreover, it was Bardella who had told others about the arrangement. This time, Issa did fire him. Discredited, he hung around DC for a while. Washington being what it is, the scandal was soon forgotten and Issa found Bardella such an effective aide that he rehired him some six months later—just not as his press secretary.

KEY TAKE-AWAYS

• The rise-and-fall-and-rise-again story of Bardella underlines Washington's solidarity with members of The Club when their sins are venial and not mortal.

• It also exemplifies the idea that anyone can make it if he or she works hard enough in the perennial tradition of the American Dream.

Chapter Nine: PERFORMING ARTS

Summary

A long-time friend of Hillary Clinton's, Richard Holbrooke was a larger-than-life foreign policy luminary with an oversized ego. He was apparently in line to be her Secretary of State had she won the presidency in 2008. At her urging, he was named by Obama as Special Envoy for Afghanistan and Pakistan. But, given the contrasting styles between his dramatic persona and the "no drama, Obama" White House, he never was able to gain real traction and influence within the administration.

The thing he needed, he thought, was a one-on-one meeting with Obama, and for that he needed to see David Axelrod, the president's chief political advisor. After he had finally corralled Axelrod into a meeting where Axelrod was noncommittal but sympathetic, Holbrooke left to see Clinton. Then he suffered from a torn aorta that required an elaborate and lengthy intervention that, in the end, did not save him.

His funeral was a grand affair in the style of Tim Russert's. By this time, early in 2011, Obama's ratings were down after having been "shellacked" in the mid-term elections. Obama critics, many in the Clinton camp, were emboldened by Holbrooke's death and it was reflected in their criticisms. They asked how it was possible that a man of Holbrooke's gifts had been sidelined.

At the funeral itself (a grand affair with President Obama and former President Clinton in attendance) lengthy eulogies were given. The contrasting personalities and styles of the Clintons and Obama were on full display. Whereas Obama was exceptionally self-contained, the Clintons were very good at empathizing and showing feelings about and for the deceased. To this was added the fact that Hillary had become a friend of Holbrooke's while Obama had not warmed to him.

While Hillary Clinton is famously tough, Leibovich humanizes her with anecdotes about how she personally cared for friends and staff who had serious health problems. He recounts an anecdote about how, while waiting to give a speech, Clinton burst into tears after having learned that her colleague Senator Paul Wellstone had died in a plane accident. She collected herself and, a few minutes later, went out and very composedly gave her speech. As an explanation, Leibovich offers the following comment from Hillary's best friend in her early adulthood: "Hillary is a person who feels herself very vulnerable, and her response is to make herself bulletproof."

KEY TAKE-AWAYS

- Luck plays a determining role in a person's fortunes. If Clinton had won in 2008, perhaps Holbrooke's fate would have lived up to his expectations.

- Survival political as well as physical is the first condition of a successful politician.

Chapter Ten: ANARCHY IN THE QUIET CAR

Summary

Bin Laden is killed the Sunday after the 2011 White House Correspondents'Association dinner. Tamara Haddad is able to get Sarah Palin to appear at the brunch following the dinner. Palin is still considered to be a possible presidential candidate. She is a big hit.

The late summer of 2011 is rough, with 9.1% unemployment and the U.S. government in danger of defaulting on its debt. At the last minute, a deal is made and default is averted.

A number of high-level Obama officials are starting to leave government and cash in on their government service. Unfortunately, the corporations they are headed for have been blamed for some of the biggest disasters to befall the United States in the immediate past. There is the former Pentagon spokesman going to work for BP; the Treasury Department Counselor going to Goldman Sachs; and Peter Orzsag, the head of the Office of Management and Budget, going to Citicorp. The Obama team's idealism is falling by the wayside as some of them scramble to "monetize government service."

Just at this time, the machinery to reelect the President is starting to come to life. However, much of the idealism and spirit of that campaign has been corrupted, or at least tainted, by the Washington culture. Obama is particularly bothered by leaks; he was very proud of the leak-free 2008 campaign. Much to his chagrin, leaks spring from a coordinating committee made up of the White House, the Chicago headquarters to reelect the President, the VP's office, and others. Obama never again addresses it.

KEY TAKE-AWAYS

- Washington changed the Obama people more than the Obama people changed Washington.

- When idealism meets the grind of daily reality, the latter usually wins out.

- The compromises that those in power make, whether necessary or not, are corrosive to the high-mindedness of those who have just attained power.

Chapter Eleven: THE PRESIDENTIAL CAMPAIGN: THIS MOVIE AGAIN

Summary

By the time 2012 rolls around, the "Candidate of Hope" has become, in Leibovich's words, the Great Delustered. A number of promises from 2008 were broken throughout the four years that followed. The promise to never hire lobbyists was broken (supposedly finessed by having that particular lobbyist in question deregister as a lobbyist after Obama's victory, even though remaining president of a lobbying company). There were two more instances of lobbyists being hired.

Meanwhile, Mitt Romney can't seem to seal his victory in the primaries. Observers marvel at how out of touch he seems; he makes comments about making $10,000 bets, and his wife driving multiple Cadillacs.

The misery of spin rooms is dissected in this chapter. No matter how well or badly a candidate does, spin doctors always say that he or she has done well.

A controversy erupts after a Politico article appears discussing the stupidity of voters.

The article rests largely on the opinions of pollsters who hold that view. Liebovich shrewdly points out that many professions disparage their clients, or worse.

A version of this thinking is attributed to the Obamas. A common theme is that the American people do not appreciate Barack Obama. In a 2008 speech, Michele Obama may have given the best expression to the Obamas' thinking in regards to the state of American voters, as well as giving voice to the unrealistic, naïve, and even arrogant hope the Obamas had of fundamentally changing voter apathy: "Barack will never allow you to go back to your lives as usual—uninvolved, uninformed."

As Romney finally gets the nomination, the summer of 2012 sees the campaign roll into full swing. A contest to see which candidate is most down-to-earth and non-elitist (the "who would you rather have a beer with" contest) is under way.

In late March, the HBO film adaptation of the book *Game Change* was first seen in the Newseum. The book and film ridicule Sarah Palin, portraying John McCain's campaign chief, Steve Schmidt, as being terrified of having her one heartbeat away from the presidency if McCain wins, even though Schmidt was the one who suggested that McCain select her. Schmidt garnered a lot of fame and money from his involvement in *Game Change.*

KEY TAKE-AWAYS

• There is "truth," and then there is "political truth." In politics, the second is the only one that matters.

• In 2008, the Obamas and their campaign believed too strongly, and too naïvely, in the potentially transformative power of their possible presidency.

Chapter Twelve: THE PRESIDENTIAL CAMPAIGN: SADDENED, TROUBLED

Summary

The 2012 Obama campaign tries to revive some of the 2008 magic as infighting within the campaign contrasts with 2008's harmonious experience. Out of the gate, the campaign fumbles with surrogates making mistakes. Biden prematurely comes out in favor of gay marriage, stealing Obama's plan to trumpet his position of also being in favor of gay marriage. Hilary Rosen accuses Romney's wife of never having worked a day in her life. Newark Mayor Cory Booker – a Democrat and Obama ally himself – says that Obama's attacks on Romney's private-equity work are "nauseating" to the American people.

After Tim Russert's death, Tom Brokaw, the elder statesman of journalism in This Town, officiated the marriage of two of the most prominent journalists in DC, who happened to work for two of the most prominent news organizations in DC, according to Brokaw: Politico and NBC. A month earlier, Brokaw had stated that attending events such as the

Correspondent's Association dinner ends up "stealing your soul."

At the time of the 2012 campaign, the country is still struggling with an 8.1% unemployment rate, and median net worth is at levels equal to those of the early 1990s. DC's economy, meanwhile, is enjoying the boom of the elections, with money pouring in to finance the media, strategists, consultants, and PACs.

Obama has grown to like Biden but is also condescendingly protective of him. The race is on to guess who Romney will pick to be his VP running mate. Romney's campaign is deeply focused on not committing a Palin mistake: no prima donnas, lightweights, or vetting surprises.

The 42-year-old Paul Ryan wins out. He adds intellectual heft, unlike some Tea Party standard bearers, while being a true conservative. He also doesn't have the burden of being an out-of-touch millionaire, and is even hip to his generations' pop culture. Romney truly seems to warm to him on the campaign trail. Ryan is lionized by his colleagues upon his return to Congress after being named candidate.

KEY TAKE-AWAYS

- In a long presidential campaign, what looks like a major faux pas may really be inconsequential.

- In This Town, power is the idol everyone worships. Even among the players, the anointment of one of their own as a VP candidate results in them falling all over themselves to get in with the candidate.

Chapter Thirteen: THE PRESIDENTIAL CAMPAIGN: BELLY FLOPS, BOURBON CHOCOLATE TRUFFLES, AND WONDERFUL RUINS

Summary

Chris Christie, the Governor of New Jersey, barges through the campaign as a typical yet original pol. After flirting with the idea of running for president, and then of becoming Romney's VP pick, he is offered the coveted keynote speaker's slot at the Republican Convention. Affecting humility, self-sacrifice, and blunt honesty, he prepares for a potential 2016 run.

The campaign sees the Comeback Kid do it again. Bill Clinton completely redeems himself after his less-than-stellar performance in 2008. He gives the best speech at the Democratic Convention—better than Obama's.

The conventions are huge smorgasbords of parties full of delicious food and expensive drink, courtesy of lobby firms. The book gives sarcastic sketches of great luminaries whose reputations have become somewhat tarnished. There is Robert Rubin, the former

Goldman Sachs executive and Secretary of the Treasury during the Clinton administration. After having presided over the late 1990s boom and eventual deregulation of the finance industry (deregulation which led to the financial meltdown ten years later), Rubin earned $126 million at Citigroup while it lost oodles of investor funds and had to be rescued by the government.

Election night rolls around with Obama on top. A poignant side note regarding Romney's campaign: As soon as the election results are announced, his Secret Service detail disappears.

Soon after, the Petraeus scandal unfolds. Patraeus is forced to resign; however, in quintessential "This Town" tradition, he and his ex-lover land very lucrative book contracts.

Axelrod is able to leverage his celebrity status to raise a cool $1 million for his favorite charity for epilepsy research, CURE (his daughter is an epilepsy sufferer), by promising to cut his moustache on MSNBC's Morning Joe if he gets enough donations.

A story by the *Times*' Jo Becker portrays Axelrod subtly criticizing Valerie Jarret, Obama's closest confidant, as being someone who took advantage of her Obama quasi-family status to have her say over and above the official meetings where issues were supposedly worked out.

Jarret appears to be perhaps the only person to wholly eschew her after-the-Obama-White-House interests, in the interests of the Obamas—or at least she is seen as such.

KEY TAKE-AWAYS

• The worlds of politics, media, and corporations come together in an incestuous embrace whereby the interests of "The People" are not paramount (and may even be a hindrance).

• In DC, the power of money makes bedfellows of even the most strident partisan figures in the interest of holding future positions in lobbying firms after officeholder tenures are over.

Chapter Fourteen: THE LAST PARTY

Summary

In December of 2012, 91-year-old former Washington Post editor Ben Bradlee, a legend in his own time, hosts a party at his mansion. There are three kinds of parties in DC: those attended by the young, ambitious, and up-and-coming; those attended primarily by the has-beens; and those attended by principals who are afraid of the up-and-coming snipping at their heels, and are also afraid of the has-beens who remind them of what is in store for them. Bradlee's party was mostly for the has-beens.

Dubbed "The Last Party," it was at first thought to be so called because of Bradlee's deteriorating health; actually, according to the Mayan calendar, the world was coming to an end and so Bradlee's wife, Sally Quinn, decided to name the party thusly.

The only high-ranking official in attendance is Susan Rice—paradoxically, after her bid to become Secretary of State, she became an object of intense attention. Rice was not given to wooing Thought Leaders, or anybody else, in soirees of this kind, which was partly why she didn't get good press . . . or the job. Attending the Last Party was too little too late.

The party and the book end as Bradlee bids farewell to his guests and, in one of his favorite phrases, "the caravan moves on."

KEY TAKE-AWAYS

• After Ben Bradlee's newspaper exposed Watergate, journalists attained celebrity status like never before in the Washington milieu.

• Even as he deftly and incisively criticizes Washington's many foibles and shortcomings, the author vastly enjoys being part of This Town and belonging to The Club.

EPILOGUE

Summary

News of *This Town*'s imminent publication elicits a response from Washington personalities that does justice to the book's reports of paranoia and insecure self-promotion. People are afraid of being both included and excluded; they want to know if they are criticized in the book, and they offer to give information about their "friends" if tiny negative morsels about themselves are omitted.

Much of the action in the epilogue takes place at two parties upon the occasion of Obama's second inauguration. Many of the usual suspects are in attendance, the food is great, and we learn tidbits such as the fact that Colin Powell would rather be called "General" than "Secretary."

The run up to this inauguration feels more like an obligation. Gone is the excitement of four years earlier. Moreover, a number of people come down with colds or much worse. George H.W. Bush is in and out of intensive care, and Hillary Clinton suffers a major concussion. Tammy Haddad's husband is sick with lymphoma.

Obama taking the oath of office at his second inauguration.
Photo Courtesy of CC

The orderly inauguration crowds are more diverse than usual, and the metro is jam-packed but runs on time. The inauguration ceremony emotionally moves Leibovich, but then he confesses that he is moved during this event no matter who is taking the oath of office.

KEY TAKE-AWAYS

• Appearances are everything in Washington, and they may hide something very different from that which is advertised.

• In spite of all the cynicism, there are moments of genuine feelings.

PUTTING IT TOGETHER

Former campaign advisor to President Clinton, James Carville has famously observed that, while presidential candidates always run against Washington and vow to change its incestuous political culture, in the end, "Washington always wins." The events of recent years have largely borne this out.

Written by an admitted card-carrying member of The Club, Leibovich's *This Town* nevertheless by and large succeeds at being objective in its depiction of the actors and situations narrated. Moreover, the author mostly avoids the temptation of settling scores or making those people against whom he might hold grudges look bad. When Leibovich out and out declares his admiration for someone (as in the case of Ben Bradlee), it is expected that he will paint a favorable picture of that person. But Leibovich criticizes Bradlee's relationship with JFK, even if he admits that those were different times.

In the end, it is difficult to discern who Leibovich really admires. He doesn't say as much about many. But does he try to surreptitiously paint certain people in a good light?

One particular instance comes to mind with Hillary Clinton, who reportedly breaks down at the news of the death of a fellow senator. Somehow it is difficult to believe that the death of a colleague, with whom she seems to have no hint of any kind of a special friendship, would elicit such a strong reaction from a person who is infamously tough. Then again, perhaps Clinton truly is sensitive, and the exterior toughness is just a practiced act. What is clear is that the whole of Washington DC often appears to be one big act put on mostly for the benefit of the actors.

Readers Who Enjoyed This Ebook Might Also Enjoy...

Mark Leibovich's _This Town_ (the full book)

George Packer's _The Unwinding: An Inner History of the New America_

Mika Brzezinski 's _Knowing Your Value_

Save Time Summaries' _The Unwinding: An Inner History of the New America -- George Packer -- Summary & Analysis_

Made in the USA
San Bernardino, CA
23 January 2014